I am KiNG!

Written By:

**E. DESMOND TAYLOR
VERNON G. YANCY**

Illustrated By:

TONI WEATHERS

I Am King!

Copyright © 2022 E. Desmond Taylor & Vernon G. Yancy All rights reserved

No part of this book may be reproduced, or stored in a retrieval system, or transmitted in any form or by any means, electronic, mechanical, photocopying, recording, or otherwise, without express written permission of the publisher.

Limitless and Purposeful (LP) Publishing

ISBN 978-1-957803-00-5 - *Hardcover*

Printed in the United States of America

I Am King! is a picture book dedicated to uplifting Black boys around the world. It is a vital component within the larger narrative of the So Organic, So Suave (SOSS®) collection, which embodies a product suite of grooming and lifestyle essentials primarily intended to uplift Black men and Black families.

This book aims to instill confidence, values, and self-esteem in Black boys through a daily self-care and grooming routine cultivated in affirmations.

The merits, instructions, and illustrations presented will not only introduce young men to an impactful self-care and grooming routine, but they will also amplify the advantages of achieving daily tasks and conquering fears with affirmations rooted in self-love.

Just before Elijah jumps out of bed to start his day, he sits up, stretches out his arms and says aloud...

I am Blessed!

Activity: List 3 blessings in your life.
1. _____
2. _____
3. _____

Elijah then rushes to his bathroom and looks into the mirror with a smile, saying, "I matter, and my image does too!"

As a Black boy, Elijah was taught by his parents that he is connected to royalty through his African roots—making him a king. And every king must take proper care of his body and protect his crown through a daily self-care routine.

Elijah turns on the sink and runs the water as he grabs the soap. He begins washing his hands and cleansing his face. Once thoroughly cleaned, he pats his face and hands dry with a towel, then reaches for his toothbrush and toothpaste and begins brushing his teeth. Next, he rinses his mouth with mouthwash and finishes by flossing his teeth. Elijah looks up, smiles and says...

I am Clean!

5 Simple Rinsing Tips:
1. Pour mouthwash into top/cup
2. Empty the cup into your mouth
3. Swish for full 30 seconds
4. During rinsing, tilt head back and gargle in your mouth
5. Spit the liquid out into the sink

3 Simple Flossing Tips:
1. Grab a foot of flossing string
2. Wrap both ends of the string around your index fingers
3. Place string in between 2 teeth and pull the floss back and forth for 3-5 sec per space

Elijah's grooming does not stop there. Just like a king, Elijah must protect his crown, inside and out. As he looks into the mirror, Elijah dips two fingers into his natural Wave Crème, massages it into his hands, and applies it throughout his hair. Then, he grabs his hairbrush and brushes through his waves. Elijah wants his crown to stay healthy and neat. As he embraces himself, he says...

I am Suave!

SUAVE [/swäv/ (adjective)] – charming, confident, and elegant (typically used of a man).

Before Elijah gets dressed, he has just a few more steps to complete.

He then applies deodorant under his arms to keep a fresh aroma. He always remembers his parents' advice: "King, it's important to stay fresh throughout the day." With that in mind, Elijah knows...

I am Fresh!

Elijah looks in the mirror with pride, remembering that the color of his skin does not define him and that he must do all he can to protect his skin. He reaches for his body butter, scoops some out with two fingers, massages it between his palms, and applies it to his skin for much-needed moisture and a nourishing glow.

As he goes through life, Elijah understands that how he presents himself to others matters, but how he presents himself to himself matters most. That is why he tells himself daily...

I am Fearless!

From all the stories he has read and movies he has seen, Elijah knows every king is clothed in majesty. He opens his closet and selects his outfit for the day, while keeping in mind who he is and what he aims to achieve.

While he stares into the mirror one final time before heading out the door, he remembers his parents telling him, "King, always affirm yourself from head to toe, as you only get one shot to make a first impression." At that moment, he nods his head and says...

I am Me!

AFFIRM [/əˈfərm/ (verb)] – to state as a fact, boldly and publicly

IMPRESSION [/imˈpreSHən/ (noun)] – an idea, feeling, or opinion about you that is received by someone else

Now that Elijah has completed his daily self-care routine, he is ready to conquer his goals and enjoy his day. Elijah holds the keys to his future, and he knows that success begins with himself. The effort he puts into grooming his body and mind each day makes him more prepared, ready, and confident.

CONQUER [/ˈkäNGkər/ (verb)] – overcome and take control of

It does not matter what neighborhood Elijah comes from or what he has or does not have. Because he only focuses on being the best that he can be, he will proudly exclaim...

I AM KING!

EXCLAIM [/ikˈsklām/ (verb)] – to shout or cry out loudly

About the Authors

Vernon G. Yancy — *"I am Limitless"*

I defined myself early in life. Born and raised in Los Angeles, California, to two parents who are unique epitomes of taking ownership of life, I knew I would not succumb to what others may have expected of me. My experiences within service organizations, such as Jack and Jill of America and Kappa League, would empower me to take control of my personal composition by evading the thought of not being able to do anything that hasn't been done before. So, after being advised otherwise, I entered Howard University (HU) to major in Mechanical Engineering.

Fulfilled from my previous experiences, I searched for opportunities to groom the next generation of leaders, and was ultimately led to establishing a mentorship program alongside Kappa Alpha Psi Fraternity, Incorporated, which uplifted at-risk young men in Washington, D.C.. Then, after graduating from HU with honors, I built a grooming haven called So Organic, So Suave (SOSS®), a premium suite of grooming and lifestyle essentials aimed at elevating one's confidence, self-care and physical image. Knowing the impact of a confident mind and a consistent grooming routine, I committed myself to uplifting people of all ages with elevated, external and internal grooming experiences. I Am King! is an exciting extension of this commitment, as I continue to prioritize helping our young boys boost their self-care, self-love, and grooming techniques.

E. Desmond Taylor — "I am Purposeful"

Growing up in Houston, Texas to a single mother who was left to raise two young kids after my father succumbed to non-Hodgkin's lymphoma, I learned early on about the importance of living with purpose. Whether it was my involvement in youth organizations such as the Knights of Peter Claver Junior Knights— where I was elected at the age of 13 to serve as Junior Supreme Knight (national president) or Jack and Jill of America, Incorporated, building self-esteem and confidence while learning leadership skills were essential in my personal development. Also, I learned the importance of surrounding myself with good mentors. As a student at Howard University, I decided to pay forward those same lessons during my involvement in student government and Kappa Alpha Psi Fraternity, Incorporated where I served as Undergraduate Grand Board Member. I obtained a Bachelor of Arts in Legal Communication with a minor in Political Science and currently studying to receive a Master of Public Policy from the Hobby School of Public Affairs. Pursuing my purpose professionally has afforded me the opportunity to serve as Senior Communications and Policy Specialist in the Office of Government Relations for Houston Mayor Sylvester Turner. I Am King!, my first published piece has reinvigorated my purpose and commitment to mentorship through self-care and grooming accompanied by affirmations. Moreover, my hope is that this book is not simply a read-along for young boys and families; rather, it is a roadmap to self-value and self-love.

www.ingramcontent.com/pod-product-compliance
Lightning Source LLC
Chambersburg PA
CBHW041412010526
44107CB00015B/1145